MW00760356

Sinatra,

THE JEEPERETTES

& me

POEMS
BY

SUSAN LEMBO BALIK

GARDEN OAK PRESS

Garden Oak Press
1953 Huffstatler St., Suite A
Rainbow, CA 92028
760 728-2088
gardenoakpress.com
gardenoakpress@gmail.com

First published by Garden Oak Press on July 15, 2014
ISBN-13:   978-1499792256
ISBN-10:   1499792255

Printed in the United States of America

In loving memory of my mom
and for my dad – thanks for the memories

and

for Maria
for helping me to banish the crow

Table of Contents

INTRODUCTION

I am honored to write an introduction to Susan Lembo Balik's *Sinatra, the Jeeperettes & me* because it is the kind of book you want to read from start to finish in one sitting, because the poems are powerful and moving, because she makes the people and places and concerns she writes about come alive for us.

These poems are rooted in narrative. She takes us with her on an evocative journey into the past of Depression-era Paterson, New Jersey, that city so connected with poetry in literary history. She tells the story of her father, whose mother died when he was three years old and because there was no one at home to watch over him since his father had to work, his older sister took him with her to school and the administration allowed him to enroll. We follow him as he grows up and, as a teenager, he must leave home, but he is indomitable. He caddies at a golf course in Paramus and lives in the caddy shack while commuting back and forth on foot to Paterson. For entertainment, he goes to dances in Paterson.

At one of these dances at the Armory on Market Street, he met his wife to be and later at St. Michael's Church, they "danced the Lindy, the Fox Trot, the Peabody." The poet paints such vivid pictures that we imagine we can see them dancing, the streets and sights of Paterson in the 1930s and 1940s lit up and shining. We imagine them traveling to see Frank Sinatra and the Tommy Dorsey Band, an image captured as though in a glass globe that glows in the light of her father's memories.

The poet's mother seems perpetually caught in the glamour of 1930s movies. Even after she had four children, she still did housework in high heels, reminds her daughter of Greta Garbo. Her routine of housework and caring for her children and cooking elaborate meals did not stop her from being elegant, small and slender in dresses and black gloves.

In *The Hour*, the poet tells how her father works three jobs to support his family as the children are growing up, often only coming home for an hour between jobs and she thinks of her father and his difficult life, as a young teen in the caddy shack "where you had to learn how/to make your own way in the world. Something I/didn't need to learn, as you were always there for me,/even in that hour." In this poem, her father comes through so clearly – hard-working, always moving forward, refusing to be defeated.

His work ethic did not diminish with age, as the poet points out in *My Father the Limo Driver*: "While the neighborhood slept, my 89-year-old father/who forgets he isn't 50, took the dog for a walk/in the early-morning dark." He falls, "cracking his forehead on the curb," but manages to get "home in time for his 5 a.m. airport run." Only after completing that job does he drive "from the airport/to the emergency room to get stitches." Moments later, "with bandaged/head and left arm in a brace," he shops for dinner: "a loaf of Italian bread, some garlic,/onions, broccoli rabe, a hunk of provolone cheese,/and with his good arm clutched grocery sack to bloody/shirt," at long last, he drives home, "to tell my mom the story."

Also, in the poem, *Life in the Fast Lane*, the poet talks about how her 91-year-old father defied the stereotypical senior: "What would/they say, if they knew his age? When most his age/are in nursing homes, he is playing/tug-of-war with a customer over a suitcase,/when most his age don't drive, he is driving/in the fast lane."

This book contains an amazing kaleidoscope of images – her parents dancing at her wedding, her mother's trip to the hospital from which she is afraid she will not return, the daughter's obvious love for her father, him for her, though both, sometimes, have difficulty putting it into words.

The poet writes about her love for her husband, their early courtship and marriage, their children, the daily rituals of life. The poet and her family are immersed in their compassion for animals and love of nature, the bird from the past she is certain has followed them from the Midwest to her next house in Hawthorne, NJ, to offer beauty and comfort. The book is also concerned with the poet's interactions with the larger world – her desire to prevent animal cruelty, the protest marches against such cruelty to which she takes her children, her concern for the environment. All are explored in this book.

The title, *Sinatra, the Jeeperettes & me*, refers to a poem about her mother and her mother's girlfriends when they were in high school. Her father says they all "heard Frank Sinatra before he was famous, took the bus to the Rustic/Cabin in Englewood Cliffs. 'Everyone stopped dancing when he sang,' he says./'Just stood there, listened. Boy, could he sing.'"

And in presenting this book and this poet, I have to say, "Boy can she sing!" These poems, the characters and places she describes – her life in Hawthorne, that Paterson suburb of her own growing up, her baton twirling – all are part of this story and it is one that opens a door into the past and memory we are drawn to enter and celebrate.

When you read this book, I think you will agree – Susan Lembo Balik is an amazing, brave poet, one worth reading and returning to again and again.

MARIA MAZZIOTTI GILLAN
Winner, American Book Award

ix

Sinatra,

THE JEEPERETTES

& me

POEMS

BY

SUSAN LEMBO BALIK

GARDEN OAK PRESS
RAINBOW, CALIFORNIA

Cheap Cologne

I was a good girl, skinny and shy. I read or sewed
while classmates hung out on street corners
or in the Lincoln School lot with the boys I had a crush on
but who never liked me back.

One December, this Italian boy who worked the pumps
a block from my house, noticed me walking
my pocket-size poodle.

"Is that a rat or a dog?" he yelled, crossing
the blacktop to get a closer look.

I fell for that line, his charm and the smell
of gasoline that clung to his uniform
like cheap cologne.

I walked past that gas station again and again.
We'd talk, laugh and I'd walk on
as though I had somewhere to go.

His name was Lorenzo and he was 17, too.
He had a twin brother and two sisters and he lived
with his very Italian family in the very Dutch town
of Midland Park, where I worked as a salesgirl
after school and on weekends.

But I told this to no one, not even my best friend,
tending my fantasy in the dark, until I found the note
with my name scrawled on it, tucked
under the windshield wiper of my brown Mustang,
until the weekend he picked me up for our date at Friendly's.

I don't remember what I wore that night or what
we talked about or what flavor ice cream I had. I do know
that his dark Italian eyes danced the Tarantella
when he smiled and that today
I still love the smell of gasoline.

Imprint

Behind white shutter doors, my teenage sister rolled
straight, brown hair around gold plastic rollers.
The size of Coke cans with holes, they protruded
like Martian antennae and left an imprint in her pillow.

At school, she traveled in a pack of sorority sisters
and dated boys – Kenny, George, then Billy,
who would twirl me in the air, my body
like confetti in his strong arms.

When it was pretty outside, they'd ride
in her '66 Mustang convertible, me in the back seat,
ice cream dripping down my chin and clutching a fistful
of wind-tousled curls from my face.

She was going to marry Billy, but they argued,
split up. Again the phone rang.
Cupping my hand to the receiver, I'd say, "It's that new guy,"
and she'd wave her arms as if batting a fly
and whisper, "Tell him I'm not home."

He must have worn her down because he was in our basement,
his cologne burning my nostrils,
my poodle keeping her distance,
as he sat uncomfortably in my dad's lounger,
waiting.

After their first was born, it started – the booze and abuse,
the other women, the leaving for months at a time
and my sister's belongings tossed on the front lawn,
their wedding picture perched on the heap.

Night after night, my mother cooked Italian-sized meals
for many mouths and we listened, but my sister always
took him back, her self-esteem battered, her stubborn will
believing, *I can fix him.*

In her ninth month, her husband left for the last time. Alone,
my sister gave birth to her fifth and to her new life,
but the abandonment made an imprint on her heart – a cut
that would heal, yet leave a scar.

Rock Climbing on Paterson Ave.

Wearing an espresso-colored housedress
that you stitched yourself,

you talk with mom in your native Abruzzese
while I fidget at the Formica table with its smooth

speckled surface and shiny silver legs.
I get up to go outside but you insist that I wait,

"Aspetta! Aspetta!" you say,
and disappear into the walk-in pantry,

then reappear with Cheez-It crackers
and Stella D'oro biscuits.

I devour the treats, then slip out to the yard
to scramble over the rocky slope,

no bigger than a sledding bump
really,

yet as a young girl,
it felt like I was climbing Mt. Everest.

The Hour

On weekdays, we saw you for an hour
between your day job at the can factory and night job
at the restaurant or the data processing plant. You walked
in the door at 5 p.m. and mom had dinner on the table.

I'd walk to the Italian deli on Lafayette Ave., squeeze loaves
of Minardi's bread until my hands hurt, then set the table,
making triangles of white cloth napkins, placing them
left of blue flowered plates bought

with Grand Union bonus points. We were careful in that hour.
Mom said you were tired, that you worked all these hours
for us. She understood you, understood that at times
you were a frightened child whose mother died

in childbirth with a younger brother, and whose father
had to parcel out some of your siblings to relatives.
You stayed with your dad, but had no one to look after you
while he worked, so your older sister brought you

to school, put you in the first grade and at the age of three,
you learned to read. When your father died, how alone
you must have felt, especially when you had to move
to the golf course in Paramus, where the regulars put you up

in exchange for caddying, where you had to learn how
to make your own way in the world, something I
didn't need to learn, as you were always there for me,
even in that hour.

In the Riverside Section of Paterson

When my dad was growing up, he lived
in a small white house on the corner
of 7th Ave. and 15th Street in the Riverside
section of Paterson. His mother died at 31,
in childbirth with a boy, who also died.
My dad was three at the time.

This house on the corner
has a garage now, but not always.
My dad says it once was a large oven,
where his stepmom baked loaves
and loaves of bread with flour and water,
yeast and salt, heat and stone. In the cellar
of the house were bottles of homemade
wine, the strong kind that made
my dad's mouth pucker, when he'd sneak
down there to take a sip.

My dad was 11 when his father died. But his
stepmom lived until she was 60. My dad
was her favorite, says my aunt. Once he cut
his wrist while caddying at the golf course
and the management gave him $200,
a fortune in the mid-1930s. He gave
his stepmom half of it.

"I guess they gave me the money
so I wouldn't sue," he says.
"But what did I know about suing?
I was just a kid."

Best Friends

The thick branch hangs low, an invitation
to climb. I pull myself up, reach even higher
until I'm sitting in the tree's inner sanctuary.

The tree still holds our energy, supports us
on its branches, where we perched like sparrows,
our dark brown pigtails – mine curly, yours straight –
bobbing in rhythm with our belly laughs.

For years we flocked to that tree and afterwards
we'd play on the swings or walk barefoot
in the creek that ran through Goffle Brook Park.
I was a year older, but you grew up faster,
leaving me behind in junior high
when you discovered boys.

I heard you are living in Florida now with your baby
and your third husband. Before that I heard
you were married to a prince who kept
you against your will in Africa,
but that story seems unreal.

Twirling Fire

At times our own light goes out and is rekindled by a spark from another person. Each of us has cause to think with deep gratitude of those who have lighted the flame within us.

— *ALBERT SCHWEITZER*

Never did get burned in those four years.
Just singed the hair on my arms sometimes,
so when I rubbed my skin, the hair crumbled
into black dust. In the middle of McKinley Ave.,
I'd practice with the other girls, my mom,
my young nieces occasionally watching
from the window, some days too hot to be
throwing a metal stick in the air, a stick
with fire breathing out the ends,
like a two-headed dragon. But there

we were in our short-shorts and bikini tops,
or tight fitting tank tops, nothing baggy
that would catch fire, no pants, no ribbons, long
hair pulled back in ponytails. I'd dip the baton's
end in a Maxwell House can I kept in the garage,
the gasoline fumes making us slightly high, hold
a Bic to the cloth soaked in lighter fluid, wrapped
carefully in layers 'til it sparked,

the flame licking higher and higher, then, I'd turn
to light the other ends. We'd twirl two batons,
do moves with names like butterfly, figure eight,
side twirl, pretzel. We'd toss one baton high,
holding the other steady in front, spin once, twice,
catch it. Then, we'd throw a flat twirl overhead

to the girl behind, and she to the one behind her,
and she to the one behind her, and so on, then we'd
all turn and repeat, as synchronized as fire twirlers
at a luau, but no Pacific Ocean as the backdrop, just
rows of houses in a blue-collar town in the 1970s,
a time when no one seemed concerned that a handful
of teenage girls played with fire on the street
with no adult supervision.

We'd only twirl fire at night games, where we'd
huddle together on metal bleachers on winter
nights, wrapped in khaki army blankets
and our dark pea coats, the ones with Hawthorne
Majorettes in big white, block letters on the back.
At half time, we'd strip down to one-piece
bathing suits, sequined and glittery
in our school colors of royal blue and white,
and march onto the football field in our white
ankle-high boots with the band and color guard
and flag twirlers. No stockings, goose bumps

on bare arms and legs, fingertips numb, all the while
I'd be running through the routine in my head, my body
trembling, partly from cold, partly from stage fright.
I'd take my place before a jumble of color and noise.
Somewhere, my parents, my boyfriend were watching.
On the white line, the batons and can of gasoline
waited. I'd begin the ritual, the baton a candle,
passing heat and light between us, the flames
rising up to sustain us.

My Favorite Things

I learned how to ski at 29,
with my friend, Rebecca. I loved to ski
but was scared of getting on and off the lift,
even just riding it made me nervous, so she
would sing, *My Favorite Things*

to distract me. I remember the lift inching along
on the steel cable, up the Green Mountains of Vermont
into an empty white-grey sky, four skis dangling
over the slope, smooth and bright
as bridal satin. We'd sail over thick swatches of fir,
spruce, and hemlock, their branches looking
as if they were dipped in vanilla frosting. I remember

how the trees shimmered like ghosts, rooted
in the mountain stillness, appearing to reach
for us, and all the while
we'd sing.

The Apartment

In my late 20s, a good friend and I decided to get
an apartment together. Until then, I had lived
home – had never even been away to college.

Though I was long overdue to be out on my own,
I was anxious about telling
my traditional Italian parents.
So I didn't.

We found a great place, close to where we worked
in Englewood Cliffs. I got the nerve to tell my mom
the night before we had to sign the contract.
I was sitting on my pink-flowered bedspread,
she standing by the shuttered closet doors
near the desk my dad built. "I thought you wouldn't

move out 'til you got married," she said. My mom rarely
cried, but her eyes were wet that night.

"But, mom, what if I don't get married 'til I'm 50?"

I don't remember her response, but the tears
she blinked back were enough
to make me stay.

Falling for an Iowa Farm Boy

You and I, Iowa farm boy and Jersey girl, first meet
in Independence amid the whir and clatter
of machinery, giant mixers dispensing
Thousand Island and Ranch into wishbone
shaped bottles that whisk along an assembly line.

On our first date, we consider the Royals win
after 16 losses, a good omen. You drive
me back to my hotel and we talk in the lounge,
or rather I talk – you were too shy or too scared
to say much. As we part, I announce
that if you ever want to see New York City, I'd love
to be your tour guide.

"When?" you ask.
"A long weekend, like Memorial Day," I say.
You leave and I wonder if I'll see you again.

In the morning, I get a message from you
from the front desk saying how much you enjoyed
the evening. Back in Jersey, I call to thank you.
You tell me you've made reservations.

"For what?" I ask.
"Plane reservations for Memorial Day weekend," you say.

I know you from daily phone calls and letters,
yet I'm anxious about The Weekend. Worry
if you'll like my coast. So I plan an adventure
from shore to city to mountains to make sure you do.

At Newark Airport that Friday evening, I wait
cross-legged on the floor. You emerge
in shorts and a blue dress shirt, the sleeves
rolled up your forearms, but your wardrobe
can't conceal awkward body language.
I'm scaring you again.

We begin our whirlwind tour at sunrise, drive
the Parkway to Exit 82, follow signs for Island Beach,
where hot sand burns our feet, ice-cold waves sting.

Saturday evening, I swap my bathing suit for an orange
sundress and heels, and you turn in trunks
for dress pants and a blue blazer. Through the tunnel,
we're greeted by a homeless man who wants to wash
our windshield, and green plastic bags heaped haphazardly
along Eighth Avenue. Your sunburned face turns pale
and I wonder, after this trip, if I'll see you again.

But the city's romantic language massages your memory
as we share wine and pasta, and I fall asleep on your shoulder
in *Les Misérables*. The next morning, we take a touristy
brunch cruise and laugh over the ship's hand, who thinks
you've run off with the cruise liner's blue blazer.

Later, hand in hand, we walk around the Met and afterwards
walk more than 30 blocks to St. Patrick's Cathedral, where
I imagine marrying you
on the grand altar.

Watching My Parents Dance

I remember my mom and dad dancing at my wedding,
he in his black tux, she in a cream-colored gown, beads
at the shoulders and neckline, gliding on the dance floor
like figure skaters, how they fit together
in this way, each anticipating the movement of the other,
after being married for 50 years. They met

at a dance at the Armory on Market Street, where my dad
asked his friend, "Who's that girl?"
"It's one of my girlfriends, Amelia," he'd said.
Later, my dad asked her to dance, but her dance card
was full, so she told him he'd have to wait 'til next time.

The next week, he saw her at St. Michael's Church, and they
danced the Lindy, the Fox Trot, the Peabody, sometimes
the Waltz. She was 17, a senior in high school; he was 19.
They took buses to the Rustic Cabin in Englewood Cliffs
and danced to Frank Sinatra before he was in
the Harry James or the Tommy Dorsey bands
and they went to dances in churches and halls
all over Paterson for 35 cents. Afterwards, they'd stop
for Libby's hot dogs, and my dad would walk my mom home
to Paterson Ave., then walk back to the golf course

in Paramus, where he caddied in exchange for rent. My dad
won my mom over. My grandma, too. "He's a good boy,
such a hard worker," she'd say, and she'd feed him
homemade pasta and meatballs and warm bread,
though my mom told her not to be too nice to him.
"It's not like I'm going to marry him," she'd said.

The Cardinal

Like a debutante in a red gown, I couldn't ignore her,
how she'd sit on a low branch, peck her hello each day
on my window, then swoop over a neighboring cornfield,
a streak of crimson against an azure Missouri sky.

Packing in late autumn, I knew I'd miss her—
how her flamboyance
upstaged sparrow and squirrel, how she'd drop into my day
at just the right moment, like a good friend knocking
on the back door when you're most in need of company.

I was in my new home just a few weeks when I heard a noise
like fidgety fingernails on a tabletop,
faint at first, then gathering
greater urgency. I looked up to see a flutter of red
at my kitchen window.

Had my old friend found me hundreds of miles away?
I wanted to believe she had. I wanted to climb on her back,
luminous as a flame, and soar over the fields of the Fox Valley,
away from this new beginning, away from this place
where I felt so alone.

Each day for years, she'd visit me, until I had to move again,
this time back to my hometown in Jersey. It wasn't long before
my dad told me he had spotted a cardinal:
"Can't remember seeing one in the yard before this."

I watched my friend flit from pine to sycamore,
her brilliance bold as a peacock's feathers,
bold as a sunrise
awakening the day.

Redefining Boundaries

for Jessie

Roses entwined in a trellis obscured
the little white house next door,
their beauty untouchable because bees drunk
on nectar threatened us
each time we passed. On the other side

lived old lady Zinzer, small and wiry,
with short grey hair, a husband, no kids
and a thick accent that spat on us.

Didn't matter how often we helped
the woman – that my dad took her to the E.R.
after a tumble down the steps,
and while her arm mended,
my mom ironed her husband's shirts.
My brother scared away a strange man
from her door at 2 a.m. When she sunk
in the cesspool, my mom pulled her out.

None of that mattered; eventually old lady Zinzer
shunned us entirely and my parents grumbled:
"Should've left her there." "Shouldn't have bothered
to help." "Should've let her sink."   But they never would.

I remember old lady Zinzer playing "radio war"
with my brother, her volume matching his
until she got him in trouble. I remember
her tattling to town hall about the building permits
my dad didn't get. But mostly I remember
that she called the cops on our party, and how
they came in for a beer, and my dad, just back
from Hawaii with my mom,
had one, too.

We got older and one by one left home.
And old lady Zinzer got older, too,
leaving the little white house for a nursing home.
When I moved back mid-life, the house hid behind
evergreens, not rosebushes,
and I met Jessie, the new neighbor – tall and sturdy
with short grey hair, no husband, no kids,
a kind heart and a hearty laugh.

Weeks later, my three-year-old went missing.
She'd let herself out the back gate,
knocked on Jessie's door and had an ice pop
in her kitchen – my daughter redefining boundaries
while I stood in the shadow of evergreens.

The trees grew gangly and crooked, so my dad
uprooted and replanted. They withered. He replanted.
They died.
He gave up.

Over the naked fence line, I could see my neighbor
reading on her deck, tending the flowers in her yard,
and with each hello,
each dog biscuit,
each jar of homemade applesauce or soup,
each story,

a friendship flourished in the space
where evergreen and rosebush
once grew.

Housework in High Heels

When you were a young bride, you did housework
in high heels, a way to feel Jackie O as you went about
your unglamorous job of raising four kids.

Every day, I watched you banish
hairballs and dust bunnies, steam wrinkles
from underwear and pillowcases edged in pink
crochet, scrub kitchen floor on hands and knees, wipe
water spots from shower stall and bathroom mirror.

Every evening, I watched you cook a treasure
trove of Italian comfort foods, spaghetti and meatballs,
eggplant parmesan, pasta fagioli and broccoli rabe
swimming in olive oil and garlic.

While I didn't inherit your flair
for domesticity, sometimes, I do see you
in me – when I walk the kids to school, sew a dress,
stand at the stove stirring a pot of sauce, sit down
with my family for dinner.

It's then I savor the simplicity and slow rhythm
of motherhood, juicy as a summer tomato
and I bow to your example.

Spirit of Playground Past

in memory of Mark Sasso

The spirited song of school children at recess
permeates the chapel where we talk of Exodus.
My gaze drifts from instructor to opaque panes,
where I see silhouettes of children
running
climbing
jumping

in utter abandon. I sense the ghost
of a man no longer encumbered
by the chains of cancer, playing
kickball and tag as a boy on this same
blacktop where I once played hopscotch
and double Dutch, too,

on this same blacktop where his children –
my children – now dangle from monkey bars
and squeal with fierce joy as they slide
through hallowed space,
freeing his spirit with their laughter,
a sound sweet and nourishing
as manna from heaven.

Along the Path

It's early August and I help you climb
into the banana-colored moving van
the one we nicknamed Big Bird. Your dad
is behind the wheel. I follow with your sister
and the dogs in our SUV pulling the U-Haul.

For the moment, you forget you're leaving
behind our next-door neighbor, your best friend,
and the others who will go on to third grade
at St. Pat's without you.

Across four state lines, our caravan crawls
in the right lane of Route 80. Cars speed past
and I feel like a donkey among thoroughbreds.
I think about our old life in Chicago, our new
beginning in Jersey and how all through spring
and summer you asked if you could walk
to your new school, but I didn't know the answer.

Now, here we are on the first day of school cutting
through the corner lot where the neighbor kids
play ball on the cracked blacktop, past the bank,
library and drug store, over railroad tracks,
past post office and local pub
to the corner where Debbie crosses us
to the brick school – the same school
I went to as a child.

Then, each afternoon, we go back again
past post office and pub, over railroad tracks,
past drug store, library and bank
through the corner lot to our door,

and all the conversations in between
about Bruce and the Beatles, the book you're
reading in Lit, how you got in trouble in gym class,
football with Mr. Wrobes and the funny things
your friends did in class

and all we discover along the way,
like the plastic Coke bottle Huckleberry clutches
in his teeth and the cherry blossom petals
blanketing our path like snow.

The Collector

Fairy and angel watch over a menagerie of misfits
in a corner of my dad's yard. Ceramic squirrel and turtle,
decapitated goose, a plastic daisy sprouting
from the dirt. All were once trash

until my dad gave them a home. Having grown up
in Paterson during the Depression, my dad abhors waste,
can't fathom someone discarding what he considers useful,
can't bear to drive away leaving it curbside. His hobby

extends beyond yard ornaments. Instead of cars, his garage
shelters picture frames, baskets, board games, bird cages,
pet carriers, coolers, lawn chairs, stereo speakers, end tables
that all fit together
like some giant jigsaw puzzle.

Alone

You sit on the carpet behind red and blue toy shelves,
moving little people and farm animals around a barnyard.
The teacher intrudes on your world, yells for the class
to clean up, get ready for storytime.

All through that fall and winter, I never understood
why I paid good money so you could play alone,
something you could do at home for free.
I guess it's what I was supposed to do – send you

to preschool when you turned three so you'd learn
how to share, make friends. In spring, you emerged
occasionally from your corner to play dress up,
puzzles, dump trucks at the sand table,

interacting with the other kids, sometimes, feeling
your way, as if barefoot on hot sand, moving
tentatively toward an ocean. It's fall again, six years
later, and you're about to go trick-or-treating

with a good friend and her friend, and you fret
about being left out of the threesome.
"But, that's okay," you tell dad.
"I'm used to being alone."

Afternoon in Paradise

A friend invites us to spend the day at her lake
in Ringwood. "The water is delicious," she raves.
So, one warm, early-September day we set out.
My picnic basket, packed with figs and apples
and hummus, sits on the back seat next
to my seven-year-old daughter. My 12-year-old son, iPod
growing out of his ears, sits next to me in the front.

Our car labors up a winding driveway and we walk up
brick steps to ring the front door bell. A half-hour
later, after a tour of the house and my friend's new
paintings and should we pile in one car or take two
and what cooler should be packed with what
and visions of my perfect picnic lunch going rancid
in the back seat of the car, because I forgot
to pack an ice pack, we drive in separate

cars to the lake. "The grass is different here
than on the island," says my friend. "Come, I'll show you."
Once she has settled on a spot, she tells her husband to take
beach towels back to the car. He fetches them, returns,
and she asks him to bring back

the cooler. My daughter, her swimsuit dry as overdone
toast, peers at mud-colored water and plops down
between picnic basket and Kadima
paddles. "It's gross," she announces.
"She's not accustomed to lakes," I say and coax
her from blanket to water, where geese droppings
drift by like rubber ducks.

Taking off

You are seven and in second grade
and your dad wants to surprise me
for my birthday by teaching you how
to ride a two-wheeler.

So, the training wheels come off
on your pink bike, the one
with the white basket
with the pink and purple flowers
on it, and he works with you over
and over again in the vacant church
lot across the street from our house.

After more than a month of practice
you take off, a sparrow nudged
from its nest, wobbly at first, dad
running alongside you, then, somehow,
you stay upright long enough
before the bike tilts
and dad catches you. I'll never forget

how you looked that day, you perched
on the banana seat, the thick
white tires on your two-wheeler
spinning over the cracks on the blacktop,
and your brown hair streaming behind you,
like the ribbons from your handlebars.

Hot Pink Rubber Gloves

I don't remember your brother
ever singing when he washed dishes, unless
moaning
groaning,
banging,
sloshing,
and rocking out to AC/DC
count.

But your kind of *Whistle While You Work* hymn,
has not been heard while he was chief dishwasher.
Never such sweet melody wafting through the kitchen,
as delicious and inviting as the smell
of just-baked banana bread.

With your blue denim apron tied tightly around your waist,
finally you're tall enough to rest forearms on the sink.
Hot pink rubber gloves,
the ones you and dad picked out special at the Rite Aid,
fit snugly on little hands, traveling up your arm
to the elbow, like some shiny imitation of formal eveningwear.

As you croon opera-like to your Disney CD, you announce
that you wouldn't mind being a maid to a princess.
I envy your gift for unearthing joy in the most ordinary task,
your ability to turn drudgery into delight,
but I know, one day, my little Cinderella,
you will dance at the ball.

The Storm

soaked through
to your Aeropostale underwear

your size 14 skateboard sneakers
squish with every step

you run to the park
in the storm
to find me
your little sister
the dogs

all the while unaware
that we'd taken refuge at a neighbor's

me sipping a latte
your sister chatting with our hostess
the dogs eating treats

The Fault Line

In the back seat, your sister babbles
to her doll, you blast the radio,
attempting to obliterate her.

"Please . . . be quiet," you beg. The "please,"
mostly for my benefit. Hands grip
the steering wheel, as I tense
for the eruption.

You're 13. Next week she'll turn eight.
Lately, you forget you were eight once, too.
The fault line snaking
between you
and her
cracks

but after three pleas, the chattering stops,
you slouch in your seat,
sing along to the Beatles.

We drive on.

Happy Girl

Before Halloween you ponder why
you never pick scary costumes.
"Happy girl, happy clothes," you conclude.

Days later you put on your poodle skirt,
the one I sewed for you, and dance barefoot
around your room. The turquoise felt puffs out

like a parasol, floats on the air and you appear
to lift off the floor as you twirl to music
only you hear.

The Season of Harry Potter

You read
lying on your belly on your bed,
legs curled under you in the big comfy chair,
on the stool at the kitchen island waiting for breakfast,
in the back seat of the car on our way to New York state.

You read
neglecting piano lessons,
your American Girl dolls,
the dogs,
your family,
your friends.

You read
steeped in the fantasy world of The Boy Who Lived,
taking Defense of the Dark Arts at Hogwarts,
zooming around the Quidditch field on a broomstick,
eating puke-flavored jellybeans.

Like tea leaves infusing hot water,
you permeate the page – the page permeates you,
until you emerge 55 days later, finishing the last of 4,100 pages
on your grandmother's couch while we celebrate
her 89th birthday, asking
that we call you Luna.

Taking the Train to Regis

In denim overalls and pinstriped
engineer's cap, you wait,
mesmerized by pulsating lights
on the tracks,
like blinking lights
on a Christmas tree
but flashier,
bigger,
better.

With my right arm I anchor
you to my side, watch the train pull into
Geneva station, watch people get off, get on,
watch the conductor wave, watch you wave back,
a big hole in your wide smile.

Years later, I'm at Hawthorne, the dog
on the passenger's seat, anticipating
your arrival – muscles quivering, wet nose
making a design on the window. I watch

a throng of commuters move instinctively
as one, like a school of fish or formation of birds.
I watch you move in your khakis and pinstriped,
button-down shirt, blending in with the 9-to-5ers.

Only your red backpack gives you away, reminds me
you're a freshman in high school, young to be riding
the train to Manhattan, young to be navigating
the subway by yourself.

I watch you break from the pack, smile as you
recognize the car, watch you stride
towards me long and smooth
to the beat of the city.

The Sandbar at Surf City

Seagulls pick their breakfast from the surf,
dip beneath the waves, rise up to a flawless sky,
reluctant crabs dangling from their beaks.
Daddies tote toddlers like sacks of groceries,

others toss a yellow Frisbee in thigh-high waves.
To get to the sandbar, we wade, doggie paddle,
occasionally kick, the whole time my daughter holding
tight to my hand. I step up

onto the sandbar. Froth dances around my ankles.
Mia catches a handful of foam, begs me to do the same.
We lie on our backs, move like crabs. A sideways
wave collides with one rolling out,

another rolling in. I lose equilibrium in these
waves. Our feet attempt to root
in the ocean floor, our hands break free
as we tumble toward shore.

The Neighborhood Prowler

Sprinting up deck steps to our Surf City beach house, green
almond-shaped eyes – so quintessentially cat – anticipate
the bowl I set beside you. You methodically

lap at edges of white 'til you have your fill.
In gratitude, you tickle
suntanned legs, your fur plush as a stuffed animal.
You leave that evening,
but reappear late morning, drink a fresh
bowl in the grey drizzle. Your tiny pointed teeth tear slices
of deli turkey and cheddar cheese, I wonder
where you've been, where you've slept,
if you belong to someone
to everyone
to no one.

Darting through the sliding glass door, you hunger
for human touch, in response purr softly, then stretch out
under the coffee table, while we watch reruns of *Jonny Quest*,
Pink Panther and *Scooby-Doo*.
Matt's right eye puffs up like a bullfrog's
and you're banished to the garage,
where Mia and I play Scattergories.
You drink more milk, then curl up in a soccer chair
to finish your nap.

When we return from dinner, you're gone and I regret
leaving you alone. I wonder
if we'll see you before leaving the beach the next day,
if the new renters will set out milk or feed you,
if you'll lick them with your sandpaper tongue,
connive your way into their living room
and their lives.

But, the next morning, I hear your persistent meow, glimpse
your trampy attitude through the screen. I wake Mia,
set out milk, offer the last turkey slices, then head
toward the beach for the sunrise, but at the corner,
we turn left and you go straight to prowl the neighborhood.
When we return, you do, too. Precariously perched
on a railing, you clean your mink-colored coat, stalk
a bird on a branch, slink along the garage rooftop
like a tightrope walker, then head back

to the neighborhood – where you belong. We head back, too,
drive the Parkway North home – where our dogs
will smell our betrayal.

Finding Your Way Home

The dogs run ahead on the path by the brook,
the same path I walked as a child. It's a warm
autumn day. Kenny Chesney plays in my earphones
and I sing along, retreating from the world.
Just beyond a tangle of trees and brush, I see Huck,

the wild one, his nose pressed to the dirt, intoxicated
by the scent of another dog that passed through earlier.
Can't believe you, who stick to my heel like gum,
are gone. I hook Huck to his leash, and climb a grassy hill
to Goffle Road, relieved you're not there dead

on the asphalt. I search the woods, retrace our path
to the field by the swings where we played, all the time
calling your name, but you're nowhere. I sprint
up steep steps, cross the street near the high school,
make a right by the wooded lot,
a left at the yellow fire hydrant,

hurry past the large inflatable pumpkin with the pop-up
black cat, all five blocks praying that someone kind has you.
Sweating, out of breath, I wave over two DPW men
working on the road near my house. I recognize one,
a classmate from high school, and yell to be heard

over his truck engine: "Did a white fluffy dog come by here?"
"Yeah," he says, "The cops just came for him." I say nothing,
run toward the house. On the steps, I hear the phone,
pant, "Hello" into the receiver. "It's the police." I know
the answer, but ask the question anyway:
"Doyouhavemydog?"

At the station, I feel like a tattered rag. A young officer
with perfect posture and movie star looks
looks me over and tells me to follow him to the back room.
You are in a kennel and I feel every bit the irresponsible
pet owner the cop thinks I am. But you

just wag your tail and I bury my face in your wooly coat.
On the walk home, I realize I never thanked my classmate,
who thought he was doing the right thing, who took you
a few feet from our back gate, where you'd have been waiting
for me to let you in.

Pet Therapy

In our Kansas City kitchen, you hide
behind my husband's legs, wearing vulnerability
and celebrity like a coat of contrasting colors
coveted by Cruella de Vil. I'm told you need a new home

or it's off to the pound. Seems the man you were gifted to
one Valentine's Day before he was married, before a newborn
took center stage in his wife's small world,
is moving out of state
without you. Your plight tears my heart into pieces,
and though we are only a month in our new home,
already have two dogs and a toddler,
I say, "Of course, we'll take you in.
Of course we will."

In our yard, your two-year-old legs race like a thoroughbred
against the backdrop of a neighbor's cornfield and at school
or the park I willingly fade into the background, as young fans
clamor to count your spots. Oblivious to the Disney machine
that made you famous, you don't understand the fuss,
but never complain of little hands pulling your tail,
tugging a black velvet ear, squeezing your neck.

More human than beast, your gentle ways make those afraid
of dogs unafraid of you. So at nine, you begin giving therapy
to the sick and lonely, waiting out days in a nursing home,
bound to wheelchairs and beds, soap operas and bingo,
apple juice and PB&J on white bread. Your magic triggers
stories of loyal four-legged friends long gone,
memories tumbling from wrinkled lips like waterfalls.

At 13 you're almost a century old. You are the senior
in need of therapy. Arthritis robs you of hikes
in the Ramapo Mountains, and I worry your hips
will give out before your heart. It pains me to see you lift
your head off the cushion when I hook up the puppy's leash
for my morning jog. On good days, though they are few,
you walk the kids to school.
The puppy chokes himself in his rush
to get there. I click his fish-line lead. He scampers ahead,
as my middle-aged legs slow to walk beside you.

Without Words

I know you're dying, but we don't talk about that
when you yelp because I touch your bad hip,
move back legs limp like paper to change a diaper,
change old beach towels soaked with urine,
wash another load at 4 a.m.

I know you're dying, but we don't talk about that
as I move the water bowl closer, support your upper body
while you struggle into position on worn elbows
to lap up the coolness.

I know you're dying, but we don't talk about that
while I cover you with my ripped *Mamma Mia* t-shirt,
hide your emaciated body from the kids and me
so we can pretend, forget you're wasting away,
because you won't eat, except sometimes hot dog buns
warmed in the microwave and honey-maple deli turkey.

I know you're dying, but we don't talk about that
while I kiss your pointy head, massage the last remaining
blubber on neck and chest, stroke the bridge of your nose
with my big toe, where a lone black spot surrounded by grey,
looks like a tiny bull's-eye.

I know you're dying, but we don't talk about that
as I stare into gentle eyes that made me fall in love
lying face to face on a tattered loveseat in Kansas City,
those same eyes that made me take you in when you were two
and needed a home.

But we don't talk about that.

The Champion

I awake at 4 a.m. to find you upright,
staring at the oversized Pottery Barn chair,
wishing your arthritic back legs worked,
or your bony body could levitate
into its velvet bosom
and really sleep.

The next morning, I find you off the doggy cushion.
You don't wag your tail or raise your head,
just look at me with sad eyes.

What kind of life is this?
I want to run like a wild mustang,
chase squirrels in the woods,
swim in a mountain lake,
jump into my favorite chair
and sleep.

I straddle you from behind, encircle
your chest in a bear hug, careful not to touch
your bad hips. Gently I lift, you yelp,
I apologize, and consider advice
I haven't wanted to hear
until now.

I awake my husband, conversation and tears spill
onto our bed covers. We talk to the kids. I make
the phone call. At the vet's office, he conceals his pity, notes
your protruding rib cage, sunken haunches, manipulates
back legs that lay limp as overcooked noodles. He thinks
you're starving yourself, eating your own body,
thinks it's time – you're just waiting for our permission.

We cry more tears, say our goodbyes. The kids leave
the room. They can't watch. The vet sticks your backside.
The needle is small, but powerful enough
to still your heart.

As if he has flicked a switch, tension dissolves
into calm, ambivalence into knowing.
You curl into fetal position. There's peace.
I stop crying.

You've been called royalty, the way you'd sit so regal,
chest puffed out, still as a statue.
You've been called champion,
and though you boast no medal, you're champion

to every child who mistook you for Perdita
and you never let on,
to every nursing home resident
who smiled on the days you served,
to every human afraid of dogs,
who you won over with your gentle spirit.

The next day I'm sitting on the shore and I imagine
you galloping across the sky, far above the waves
that swell and tumble to earth.

Run like the wind, girl.
Run.

The Ceremony for Daisy

Sometime that morning, while Daisy lay dying,
after we'd talked and cried about putting her down,
after my neighbor had left, reassuring us,
we were doing the right thing,

Mia opens her Communion Bible
and reads a passage about the Resurrection.
Then, she says she'll plan the ceremony
and closes the book.

All the rough-edged anguish from earlier that morning,
all the pleading – *No, Mamma, we can't* – has dissolved
into a comforting rhythm, a ritual. I envy
her acceptance, the decision still somersaulting
in my head.

At 1:30, Dan and Matt carry Daisy on her rectangular cushion,
down two flights of stairs as I gather extra diapers, towels,
her burial shroud – a tan sheet with tiny red flowers. I change
her wet diaper in the car's back seat, arrange Mia beside her,
and climb in front reaching my right arm back at an awkward
angle to hold her in place.

Somewhere on Union Boulevard, the cushion tilts, she slides,
yelps, struggles against gravity, My nerves, taut
as guitar strings, the commotion escalating
with each yelp, but somehow we make it to a side street
where we lift Daisy onto grass. A dark-haired stranger
stares from her driveway, watches me change Daisy's diaper,
toss soiled sheets in the trunk, wipe car carpeting as best I can,
watch Dan rearrange Daisy in the back seat,
better this time. I notice

the woman still staring and wonder what she thinks
of us, of the skeleton dog on her lawn, the whirlwind
of activity swirling in the stifling July air like a swarm of bees.

We arrive at the vet's office and Dr. Buchoff says he's ready.
Dan and Matt carry Daisy in and we all sit on the floor
around her, forming a lopsided circle, waiting
for the vet's verdict, relieved he owns
this decision, too. We take turns, murmur
into Daisy's black velvet ear.

Matt wasn't sure he wanted to come, but he is here.
He is nearly six-feet tall, nearly as tall as his father, I forget
sometimes he is only 13.

"Take care of Mia," I tell him and he takes his sister
into the reception area. They return minutes later,
see Daisy curled into fetal position on the floor. She is still.
I breathe for the first time that day.

Back at the house, Dan and Matt dig a ditch in a corner
of the yard beneath a big tree, lower Daisy into the hole
and cover her with dirt. We assemble in a semicircle
in front of the grave, while my parents look on
from the patio. Mia opens her Bible
and begins the ceremony.

The Mare

You are in the ring at the stables
and Joey canters clockwise fine,
but when you ask him to go
counterclockwise he goes to the fence
and stands there. He does this over
and over again and you are frustrated,
but Carol, the instructor, says in the wild
the herd looks to the mare and so you
need to be the mare for Joey and I have

a vision of you with your chestnut
mane blowing in the wind, galloping
across the plains in Wyoming or Montana
or Idaho, a free spirit, moving faster
than the river, clear and muscular, a blood
orange sun in a big sky and a herd of wild
mustangs with long graceful legs
thundering behind you.

A Midnight Encounter

To some you're a nuisance – dirty,
something to be exterminated,
never somebody

like I think of you, like a pet,
but one I don't have to take care of –
well, not intentionally –
though sometimes I leave behind scraps
in the garbage that should go in the compost bin.

Sometimes I worry when you're not around for a while,
because most nights I hear you scampering
in the walls, under the sink.

Sometimes I even catch a glimpse
of you scurrying along the baseboard
or through the space
between the cabinets and the hardwood floor,
squeezing under the stove.

You are black, hairy, a little bigger than my thumb,
so why do I startle
when I see you, your stealthy movements
cause me to shriek, no matter how irrational.

Then, there's the time I really got to know you.
I was on the kitchen stool at the island
and you tentatively approached
Shaggy's food dish, then scampered behind his cushion,
then halfway to the dish, back to the cushion
to the dish
to the cushion
to the dish.

Finally, you had the courage to perch
on the metal rim of the bowl. I sat transfixed,
my midnight bowl of cereal in front of me,
spoon poised in midair, while you munched
on the dog's leftovers.

Idling

Outside the brick school, I approach
an old van, dented, dirty, the air around it heavy
with exhaust. In the driver's seat a lump
of a man, middle-aged, unkempt, resigned,
depresses a button, reaches for a flyer.

"My daughter has asthma," I say.
"This isn't good for her."

"I have asthma, too, and my wife is cold," he tells me,
though there's no wife in the car.

"Please turn off your car," I try again.
"Mind your own business," he says.
I stuff frustration in pockets already full
and, like a good Catholic girl,
keep my mouth shut. Instead,
I shoot him the "Iowa stare,"
a look my husband reserves for drivers
who cut him off on the highway.

To this man, I'm a mosquito he can't squash,
so he gives in, turns off the engine, presses a button.
Glass slices through our shared air.

Walking away, I glance over my shoulder;
his van is running again. I think
of my daughter's chest heaving, trying to suck in
enough air, and I imagine oxygen masks
as the next hip accessory,

like skull caps or nose rings fashioned
from our own indifference.

On the Class Trip

He's a churchgoing man
who paints houses during the day. He likes
to jog, ride his bike, lift weights and watch Fox News.
Ten years ago, his wife left him
because she fell out of love.

It's autumn. I'm in his SUV on a class trip
with a bunch of teenagers,
talking about the precarious state of the ocean.
He tells me the fish
won't be extinct in 2050, as I've heard scientists predict,
because new species will evolve and I think

when the fish die off from overfishing and a toxic, acidic ocean
and these new species rise up, what type of Frankenfish
will they be, born of our pollution,
and will our children's children
never know the dolphin or the whale?
Then, our conversation turns

to global warming and he insists that's a hoax, tells me oil
is the lifeblood of this country and that the polar bears
aren't really drowning. "That's something made up
by environmentalists," he says.

Shared Energy

My 10-year-old daughter slumps over
her magazine. On the pages
are pictures of sheep, goats, cows
and other rescued animals living
at a sanctuary in upstate New York.
Her breathing is thin. I wonder,
if she is well enough
to go to school.

"How are you?" I ask. "Fine," she says,
absorbed in a story about Theresa,
a one-eyed cow. Her asthma
has been bad for weeks and she looks
like a china doll that might break
if handled the wrong way. "Your breathing,
how is it?" I ask, more worried this time. Finally,
she looks up at me. "The animals," she tells me,
"They're suffering."

Mornings at Farm Sanctuary

A rooster heralds in the morning as a village
comes to life. I consume each delicious detail
as if it were my last meal, hear a tractor rumble
near clusters of orangey-red
barns on the hill, a thick mist, like the frothy
head on a beer, blankets
a field of wildflowers behind our cabin.
I breathe in air, crisp as an apple. Cows graze

lazily in the pasture, while pigs root for grassy bulbs
or lay in beds of straw waiting for a belly rub.
Sheep head to the hills, sticking to each other
like chewing gum, and goats with triangular
beards and wise slanted eyes impart the stories
of those who have lived on the edge of extremes,
who have known cruelty and confinement
to fully know this bliss.

Daphney

My teenage son pulls blades of grass and offers
the treat palm up to a bunch of turkeys. Good-natured
big-breasted birds with top beaks shorter
than the bottom – sliced off
with a hot blade on the industrial farms
where they were rescued. One turkey,
named Daphney, had her fill and began chasing
my son around the barn, gurgling loudly, moving toward
his legs and trying to peck at them whenever he backed away.
My son runs for the wooden gate and Daphney sprints
to keep up, her chest jiggling like gelatin,
her whole being fixated
on her six-foot-three soulmate.
"I've seen them get attached," the guide says,
"but this is something special."

Complicity

When the steakhouse went out of business,
the new owners got rid
of the plastic steer out front, a fixture
in my hometown since before I was born.

It was big as a real steer, and gold. Tacky
like inflatable Santas in snow globes – those holiday
lawn decorations so popular now.

Across town, another life-sized cow stands
outside a small market. This one is a Holstein.
Its paint chipped, a thick rope
dangles from its neck.

A Thumann's truck pulls into the lot.
I feel the cow's eyes look through me,
as I hurry across the blacktop
to the house next door.

At the Fur Protest

1.

A small elderly woman, her spine
bowed with the weight
of the world, approached me,
sorrow drowning in the deep
wrinkles of her face.

"Get a life," she snapped,
before being sucked
into the crowd on this grey
January day.

2.

At the intersection of 34th and 7th Ave.,
a swarm of shoppers head
for the most commercial of institutions
on the blackest of Fridays.

Chatter stops, eyes grow round as plates
as people slam into a big screen TV
showing foxes, chinchillas, minks,
even dogs and cats, brutalized
and skinned alive. Some gasp,

others burrow faces in scarves,
pretending not to see the protest signs,
like the one of a model in a slinky black dress,
a fox skin, raw and bloody, draped

around her neck and over her shoulder
like a sari, its head, its sunken eyes
resting on her hip.

3.

My Black Friday ritual involves a store,
but also peace boots, long underwear, a bulky
sweater, a big screen TV and taking the train
into Manhattan with my kids.

There, shoulder-to-shoulder, we slide like lava, pulled
along with the masses toward Macy's. The video
is already playing, the one my daughter and I can't
watch, though we hear the moans – desperate, frightened
sounds that make my stomach clench.

We are early and 100 people have already gathered,
holding high signs, ready to give us a pamphlet
'til we motion we are here to protest. We take
our place behind the barricade, opposite
the string of officers in their pressed
blue uniforms and caps, billy clubs
dangling at their sides.

I look for a poster for my daughter, see one
with a picture of a raccoon that says, "He needs
his fur more than you," but decide on one
with a bunny. "Don't kill my mommy," it reads.
I grab one with a mink, its body caught in a steel trap.
My son likes to hand out pamphlets. It is something
he is good at, even the organizers comment on how
he talks to the shoppers, gets a leaflet into almost
every hand. Someone hands me a bullhorn,
and though I am shy, I lead the chanting:
"Compassion is the fashion, don't buy fur."
"Hey Macy's, what do you say? How did you get

your fur today? Gassing, trapping, anal
electrocution," and I look at my 13-year-old
daughter, chanting along with me, and wonder
what she thinks of that.

Hunting Jersey Black Bears

People protest in Mendham and Trenton, assemble
in the woods on cold December mornings, phone
the governor's office, write letters, uncover secret
meetings and reporting discrepancies,

file a lawsuit. In the end, it doesn't matter.
The black bears are shot anyway, 600 of them
the first year and hundreds more the next year
and the year after that, even though

a big majority in Jersey don't want these hunts,
even though the Fish and Wildlife Service neglect
to enforce the latching of lids on trash cans,
a nonviolent way to keep the bears away,
even though the black bears are illegally

baited with bagels and donuts, lured from dens
in Sussex and Warren and northern Passaic County,
even though humans decided to build houses in the woods,
then more houses and more houses, even though

the black bears were there first.

The Live Market at Christmastime

On the busy West New York sidewalk, we arrange
plastic chickens and butcher knives splattered
with red paint. A Spanish girl, about 15, leans
against a storefront window, head bent, plucking
her cell phone, her curly black hair obscuring
her face. Above her, a sign reads: Marzigliano's
Live Market. Behind her: cages stacked
high with restless hens, mouths stretched
in silent squawks. She approaches, asks
what we're doing. I give her a pamphlet.
She skims it, tells me she is vegetarian
about two months now, that she is the only one
in her family. She lowers dark eyes.
"I'm here for my mother," she says. I reassure
her, hold out pamphlets to passersby. Some take
them, some wave me away, some

ignore me, heads down. An older woman emerges
from the market, a black garbage bag tied at the top
in a knot; full and heavy, it dangles at her side
like a sack of presents. "Vámonos," she says
to the girl, who follows her home
to prepare for Christmas dinner.

The Greatest Show on Earth

A boy about four tugs on his mother's arm. She coaxes
him forward. He doesn't budge. Breaking free, he runs
to where we're kept – behind a metal barricade, pacing
like tigers at the zoo. We hand the boy a coloring book,
his mom a pamphlet. "I didn't know," she says.

A man comes over with his five-year-old, tells how
as a young boy he fashioned sling shots out of paper, elastic
bands and needles and shot cats in the eye. His little girl
covers her ears, begs her father to stop talking. Another
man munching popcorn from a box with a cartoon
elephant on it, asks, "How is it different

from owning dogs?" Speeding up Rte. 17, I put distance
between me and the circus, try to erase
the video images of trainers beating chained elephants
with bullhooks, electroshocking them, making them stand
on the backs of other elephants and now that the "Greatest
Show on Earth" is over, send them back to the basement
of the arena, only to go to another city tomorrow
to begin again.

Five-Year-Old Wisdom

A dead deer lies on the side of the winding
road that leads to our house in the Fox Valley.
Another half mile, I swerve,
miss a raccoon that's belly up, its guts
smashed on hot tar. I look away,

make the sign of the cross. In the back seat,
my son says, "If everyone rode bicycles,
there'd be no dead animals."

Big House on the Prairie

Another cookie-cutter McMansion stuffed
into a tidy row with its lone, wisp of a tree
sprouting from a manicured lawn.
Its flat yard, imprisoned by a white picket
fence, is smaller than the kitchen
filled with party guests, who interrupt
mouthfuls of hors d'oeuvres to gush over
shiny appliances,
granite countertops
and decorative floors that separate
designer heels from earth
once plowed by a green tractor.

What the Sea Swallows

My cousin's husband took a cruise
to Catalina and jumped
overboard.

He'd been depressed,
had another woman.
Bloggers speculate
he may have run away.

No body
has been found
and the sea won't tell its story.

On the opposite coast, I stare
into a moody sky, steel grey
washing-machine waves
enveloping a narrow beach
far up to the dunes.

The next morning, the sand is littered
with all the angry sea had spit out –
a granola bar wrapper,
gobs of seaweed,
a lavender tampon applicator,
and desperate shellfish clinging
to the inside of a red plastic cup.

The Quiet

I love the quiet
of the woods on a weekday

of my kitchen at 4 a.m.
when I'm perched on a stool writing

of a roomful of yogis
on brightly colored mats meditating

There, I slip into the quiet
like a cozy sweater or a faded pair of jeans

But this small town quiet was different – it followed
me like a swarm of gnats into the Iowa nursing home

where I walked past bunches of purple lilacs, anticipating
the visit with my father-in-law

where I welcomed the drone of the TV in his room,
a distraction from the sharp angles of his face, skin stretched

over bone where he lay dying in a hospital bed,
his once able farmer's body now limp like a spent corn husk

Illumination

in memory of Louie Balik

In summer, my daughter's bedtime is elusive,
like the fireflies she tries to contain, their lights flickering
and dodging her tentative fingers.

I let her push the edges of the night, 'til mosquitoes
drive us indoors to read. Nearly finished
with my book, the bulb in my bedside lamp pops.
We lie in darkness.

I yank the chain to the ceiling fan. Blades slice
close to my head, the lights harsh.
I miss the cozy glow of my lamp – its burned-out
bulb a warning

of what was to come – for illumination would be fleeting,
the lights blink, then go out. We retreat
to my daughter's room, where we hover
by the light like moths.

My husband comes home, swaps bulbs, but can't explain why
the fan works yet the lights don't.

"Louie," he says, and I remember that the week before,
he'd told his dying father to give a sign
that he'd made it all right.
"Blink a light, Dad," he'd said.

The next morning, my husband pulls the chain.
There's light.

My Father the Limo Driver

While the neighborhood slept, my 89-year-old father,
who forgets he isn't 50, took the dog for a walk
in the early morning dark.

He passed the big brick apartment building and crossed
the street near the tailor's shop. The dog yanked the leash
and he fell, cracking his forehead on the curb. Truck lights
rounded the corner and he scrambled onto the sidewalk,
making it home in time for his 5 a.m. airport run.

I was in the upstairs apartment, could have driven him
to the emergency room and his fare to Newark,
but he didn't want to bother me, so he put the dog
inside the house, slid into his black Town Car and took
back roads from Hawthorne to Franklin Lakes.

Staring at the back of my dad's head, the customer,
half-asleep, didn't notice the blood splattered
on the front of my dad's white golf shirt or the red tissues
wadded up on the passenger's seat,

or the gash above his left eye, turning his eye socket,
cheekbone, half his face, the color of an eggplant,
or his swollen wrist or the cracked ribs that ached
each time he breathed.

My dad's job done, the fare paid, he drove from the airport
to the emergency room to get stitches, then with bandaged
head and left arm in a brace went to the market
to pick up a few things: a loaf of Italian bread, some garlic,
onions, broccoli rabe, a hunk of provolone cheese

and, with his good arm, clutched grocery sack to bloody
shirt, and drove home
to tell my mom the story.

Too Young for the Nursing Home

Before the piano recital, I ask my 90-year-old father
if he'd like to come with us.

"It's at Van Dyke's Nursing Home," I say.

He shakes his head, tells me, "No way!
They might keep me."

That afternoon, Mia plays *Ode to Joy*
and *Legend of the Buffalo*.

Matt does *Hey Jude* and *Hallelujah*, a jazz piece.

Others play Mozart, Beethoven,
someone even does Coldplay

and my mom elbows my dad in the ribs
to keep him awake.

Life in the Fast Lane

My daughter and I watch an elderly man
with a walker. "We don't have an old
grandpa," she says. "He can walk,
he works, he drives a car."

At 91, my father still takes his Town Car
down McCarter Highway to terminal C,
the West Side Highway to the theatre district,
the Parkway to Atlantic City, while his companion

gnaws a bone on the passenger seat, customers sip
coffee, listen to him rail
on Republicans. What would

they say, if they knew his age? When most his age
are in nursing homes, he is playing
tug-of-war with a customer over a suitcase.
When most his age don't drive, he is driving
in the fast lane.

Love Poem to My Father

Dad, I see you lying on the cracked vinyl couch
in the basement, reading a thriller you've taken
from the library without checking it out, saying,
"I'll bring it back. I always bring it back."

You don't look up when I come in, though I've called
to you, your hearing so bad, those free hearing aids
you got from the VA don't work. Finally, when
I'm almost on top of you, the one white shelter dog
squeezed next to you, his fat pink belly exposed,
you look up at me and I tell you about some program
at the library I'd like to take you to and I can't help
but notice how thin you are, how your hands tremble
just a little. I look at you lying there

in your grey sweat pants and V-neck cashmere sweater,
the one mom bought for you. I look at you and can see love
in your eyes – or is that just what I want to see, what you
have such a hard time putting into words, what I have
such a hard time putting into words. I wish I could tell you

what I've been wanting to tell you for the past few years,
since we had that big argument, when I told you I hated
you and you told me you'd take that to your grave,
and though I hated you in that moment

that emotion fizzled as quickly as the firecracker
that exploded out of me, because I'm Daddy's Little Girl,
the devoted one, the obedient one,
and I don't know how to do anything else,
be anything else,
I only know how to love you.

My Mother's Mahogany Dresser

I see you in your bedroom, the four white
walls, the mahogany dresser, you fingering
the grain of the wood, as deep and dark
as the emotion in the room. You linger,
afraid you may never see this piece
of furniture again, this dresser

you and dad bought 67 years ago, when
you were newlyweds, afraid you may never
see the things it holds – the Virgin Mary statue
I bought you one Christmas, the crystal perfume
bottle, the Waterford picture frame with Mia
as a baby, grandma's embroidered handkerchiefs.
They're all there, keeping vigil.

"Come on, Mom. It's time to go," I say,
as I gently guide you toward the living room,
where dad is waiting
to drive you to the hospital.

Browning Leaves

I toss the baton overhead, spin,
catch it,
before it falls to earth.

I look to you for applause, a smile,
any acknowledgment,
but you are bent over browning leaves
that you're raking meticulously
into a pile on the brick patio.

Without lifting your gaze, you say,
"You should teach baton."

Months later, you're in the hospital tethered
to tubes that carry food and medicine
into your 87-pound body.

Your breathing is labored, like you've been climbing
a hill. You haven't the energy to talk, shift your body
in bed or lift your head from the pillow.

The doctor doesn't think you'll make it
through surgery. I, too, have my doubts – I've never
seen you like this
and it scares me.

A month later, I visit you in rehab. You're sitting
in a wheelchair eating green gelatin and drinking coffee.
You ask me why you're in this place and what
you have to do to get out.

You can't remember your trip to the ER or why
you needed an operation, yet a random memory surfaces,

like a tulip pushing through dirt, and I hear you say,
"You should teach baton."

Watching *Oprah* with My Mom

On the steps outside, I see you through the long porch
windows, sitting in the wrought iron chair with the stiff
turquoise cushion, the same chair you sit in every day.
From behind, I can't tell if you're asleep, your head bent
to the side, heavy in your hand,

your elbow set on the metal armrest – a pattern of vines
and leaves covered in chipped white paint. The TV is on,
basketball again. But you hate basketball. I pause
on the steps. So much easier to go up

than down, where I'll have to face you, face the way
you are now. You look up when I come in, your hair
flattened in the back from resting against the chair,
a swath of grey showing at the roots. You know
who I am, but your memory is not what it was.
Like the lattice armrest, pieces are missing. You smile,
and I think how much I miss you – miss you standing
in the kitchen that smells of sautéed garlic and onions
and olive oil, sauce and meatballs simmering
on the stove. I miss you crocheting blankets, telling me
about the latest celebrity gossip from *People* magazine
or who should win *Dancing with the Stars*. I miss how
you'd dress with so much style, how you'd talk about
your boyfriends in high school and how you danced
the Fox Trot and Peabody with dad at clubs
where Frank Sinatra sang. I miss you listening
to my stories with the same attention as if I'd said
I won the lottery, and how you'd always protect me,

the youngest. I think how for the last year and a half
I've been losing you piece by piece
and how selfish I feel for missing all of you,
all that you used to be.

"*Oprah* is on," I say and, like every day, you seem surprised,
though you always watched *Oprah* every day, started dinner
early so you could watch her. I talk about my job, the kids,
how you're feeling, what you had for lunch, but mostly
we watch *Oprah* in silence, the sun waning
through the long porch windows.

In This Moment,
I Feel Like Greta Garbo

At your funeral, people look at photos of you
as a teenager with your chic hairstyles
and your handbags that match your outfits,
you on a trip to Washington D.C. posing in front
of the Lincoln Memorial in a smart seersucker suit
and heels, your hand resting
on my shoulder, you as a grandmother reading
Stellaluna to my daughter. "You look so much like her,"

they say. I shake my head, think about the woman
you were – kind, classy, unselfish, content to be a housewife
and mother, never needing to be more, though you could
have been anything you wanted to be. I slip on

your black gloves, smooth against my skin, the scalloped
edges ending half way up my forearms, slip
on your black car coat, which falls to my knees, straight
and slim, button the middle button, tie

your crimson scarf around my neck. In this moment,
I feel like Greta Garbo, like Elizabeth Taylor.
In this moment,
I feel like you.

At the Poetry Reading
at the Italian American Club
in Kinnelon

I was introduced to a little Italian woman
in her eighties, about five feet tall, 100 pounds,
her hair fresh from the beauty parlor.

She was dressed smartly, all in black, a jacket
with ruffles around neckline and sleeves, a diamond
ring and gold bracelet glittered

as her hands spoke the language, a slight Dowager's hump
rose like the moon from her back. She reminded me
so much of my mom, I wept

openly in this roomful of strangers as if it were the most
normal thing to do. I wanted to keep this little Italian
woman close, listen to her voice, powdery

and light like Pizzelles, I wanted to breathe in
this little Italian woman, her calm, her warmth, her energy
enveloping me in the best Italian hug
I've ever had.

At the Graveyard in Totowa

Every Sunday morning at 10:30 my father,
who is 94, goes to the graveyard
with his three white dogs. Sometimes,
I go, too. He points

to the bare neighboring plots, neglected
like some shuttered-up building. He points
to our family plot crowded with petunias,
geraniums and spiked grass, lovingly

planted for my mother. He points to where
his name is etched into smooth, grey marble,
next to where my mother's name is etched,
and every time he tells me,

"That's where you bury me. You just have to
add the date," as if it's as effortless
as adding a date to the back of a photograph
or to a journal entry, and every time I think,

Do we have to talk about this? and every time
I put my arm around him, give his shoulder
a squeeze and say, "Dad, you're going to live
for a long, long time."

Swimming at the Great Falls

Back in the late 1920s, when my dad was in grade school
in Paterson, he'd go swimming with his friends
at the Great Falls. The water ran
in different colors, he tells me,
and he would dive off the rocks into the tepid
river, a swirling stew of white foam and red or emerald
or yellow, depending on what they were dumping
from the dye house that day. Today, the Passaic River

looks cleaner than it was back then, even though it never
looks clean to me, not the way
a river in Vermont or Colorado looks,
and I don't ever think to swim in it,
but I understand the allure
the river must have held for my dad and his friends,
the adventures they must have had under that towering
arc of water and how amazing it is that he is alive
at the age of 95 to tell me about it and how he remembers
the details as if this all happened yesterday.

The Jeeperettes

In Central High School in Paterson,
my mom belonged to a secret
club, called The Jeeperettes, with her friends
Izzy, Viola, and Margie.

"I don't know where the name came from," says my dad.
"Not like anyone had a jeep,"
not in the late 1930s anyway, when they dated,
when owning a car, even a broken down one, was a luxury.
In those days, my mom and dad walked everywhere –
to dances at the Armory,
the basement of St. Michael's Church –
took a bus to The Meadowbrook,
where for a $2 cover charge, a fortune in those days,
they heard Frank Sinatra with Tommy Dorsey,
took a bus to the Rustic Cabin in Englewood Cliffs
to hear Sinatra before he was famous.
"Everyone stopped dancing when he sang," my dad says.
"Just stood there, listened. Boy, could he sing."

My mom is dead three years today.
I wish she were here. I'd ask her
about The Jeeperettes, where the name came from,
what they did, what they talked about.
Did they talk about that guy, Mike, the one she was dating
when she met my dad, the tall, good looking one
who had lots of girlfriends, who couldn't commit?
Did they talk about why she wrote to my dad in June 1943,
while he was in the Air Force, a medic working
with Dr. Harwell, when she told him to get a furlough,
told him: "We're getting married on July 17th,"
even though they'd never talked about marriage before,

even though my dad had never proposed.
"There was this attraction," he says.
"Do you know what I mean?"
Then he hesitates, says: "I guess you do."

Today, I wish my mom were still here
so I could ask her who was this forward woman,
this bold woman, this woman who knew what she wanted
and went for it, who fell for my dad,
who is still surprised after all these years
that she picked him.

Rain on a Tin Roof

I can still hear the sound of rain
on a tin roof, the one my dad put up
50 years ago, even though
it's been months since it collapsed
in the winter storm, even though
the mangled metal
has been carted away.

I can still hear the drumming
that lulls like white noise, hear
the pinging that pelts the canopy,
so melancholy, so relentless
it can wrap me in grey, pull me
to my center like a good book,
a meditation,
a prayer.

I can still hear the sparrows' sweet
song, the ones that nested
in the corner of the rafter, see
the babies that didn't make it
all those springs when I was young,
how I'd avoid their broken
bodies splayed on the brick patio.

I can still see the one that survived
that February night, how it
hopped among snow drifts
and sharp tin, confused,
wondering
what had happened
to its home.

Channeling

I feel her running barefoot
through my blood

a river of crushed grapes
beneath stained feet

I feel her in the shiver
of wind rustling olive branches

abundant with promise
ripe with hope

I feel her as my body, my bones
dissipate

channeling her essence
into moonbeams

that catch in the light

In the Chapel at St Marguerite's

1.

My favorite moment of this day is being in this chapel
in Mendham with the sisters of St. Marguerite's
and the black and white dog, Jenny, who was rescued
from down south where someone used her for target
practice. So trusting now, she comes into my pew looking

for affection. I bend down, scratch her behind the ear.
A sister across the way plays the flute, so accomplished she is,
how the music colors this room—lavender, sky blue, and gold;
the dog leaves me, enters the flute player's pew, half way
through she has the awareness to stand, letting

the dog pass, never missing a note,
and I think about my daughter,
who is turning 12 this summer and is learning to play the flute,
who I miss so much on this retreat, my daughter who I wish
was here to lean her head on my shoulder and hold my hand
as she does during mass at home, who links her arm in mine

when we walk on the sidewalk outside church, my daughter,
the one my mom called "the happy girl," who I can feel now
in this chapel, floating on this melody, swirling around me
like a long flowing scarf.

2.

As the snow falls at St. Marguerite's, I make my way
to the chapel in the convent, where the sisters
are having 7:30 a.m. service.

Jenny, the rescue dog, is recuperating from hip surgery
and is curled up on the carpet near the back pews. She stirs
when the flutist begins. I wonder
if the sound hurts her ears, as it does my Jack Russell,
who whines inconsolably when my daughter plays
the flute at home. Toward the end of the service, we gather

at the altar, not noticing that Jenny has followed us
until she is sitting at the center of our semicircle, flanked
by five sisters dressed in long black habits, myself and another
guest from the retreat house. I cup my left hand over right,
and Jenny yawns wide, her long tongue unfurling
like a rolled up rug, as the head sister places the host
in my outstretched hand.

The Perfect Prison

On a trip to Hawaii, my husband and I visit a remote
island off Maui called Molokai. Below the steep sea cliffs,
2,000 feet high, on the north side of the island, is Kalaupapa,
a small peninsula surrounded on the other three sides
by the Pacific Ocean, making it
the perfect prison.

Even though leprosy has been eradicated for over 70 years,
a few dozen residents remain. They are free to go, but since
this colony has been their home for a very long time,
they prefer to stay. It is believed

that leprosy was first brought to the islands in the mid-1800s
by Asian immigrant workers. Shortly after, the authorities
began visiting schools, banishing
anyone with a rash or skin condition to the peninsula,
the parents informed afterwards, never to see

their children again. I think of my own son, who had acne
in his teenage years, and how
I would feel if one day he was taken
from school, imprisoned on an island and what cliffs
I would climb, what ocean I would swim
to be with him again.

The Monkey Bars
on the Road to Eagle

The metal bars glint in September sun as you climb
the wooden ladder. Lips pressed, you reach
for the first bar, smooth under your palm. You hesitate
before bringing your other hand to meet it. You hang there,
long arms, long legs, suspended in space.
We wait. You reach

for the next bar, but there's no momentum in your gangly
boy body, no cosmic pull, no amount of mother's wishing
to get you through the other rungs. My breath hitches,
as your rock feet hit earth, and feel your frustration,
as plain as the dirt and sweat on your reddened face.

Here in this field hugged by thick oaks and maples
and pines, here at your first scouting campout
with your new pack, I wait for frustration to give way
to tears, but you surprise me. You look at no one,

not me, not the Cubmaster, not the boys, especially
not the boys. You walk to the back of the line, wait
your turn as the others, nimble and compact, confident
in their athleticism, pluck each bar like a guitar string,
arriving at the last with little effort; all that is missing
is the triple dismount. Now, it's your turn,

the anticipation is palpable. Somewhere low
the chanting begins, building until everyone is cheering,
"Go, Matt, go! Go, Matt, go! Go, Matt, go!" You reach out,
hold on, one hand, then two, rock to the next bar,
yes, you have rhythm,

and suddenly you're in motion. I don't remember if you
made it to the last rung, what I remember is the kindness
in the field that day and the determination,
that later got you through all those late nights
and long commutes to New York City,

got you through the teenage *Who am I?* moments,
and though it sometimes seemed impossible,
you made it through, yes, my beautiful, determined son,
you're an Eagle, and to that I say,
"Go, Matt, go."

Moon & Back

When my children were young, I enjoyed reading
to them *Guess How Much I Love You*, a picture book
about a nut-brown hare and his son who try
to outdo the other in their love for each other.

At 13, my daughter, though she hasn't read this book
in years, still loves this game, each I love you
an invitation to reach to the moon,
the stars, the galaxy or a recent favorite,
"to the realm of my imagination," and back.
"That's very far," I'd say, quoting the main
character in the book, and letting her
win that day. My 95-year-old father

now plays this game with me, though I'm sure
he has never heard of the children's book.
It wasn't always this way. Though I never doubted
his love for me, for years, it was a one-sided
declaration. Yet, still I'd say the words

each time I'd leave him, with no expectations.
After all, I'd tell myself, he grew up during a time
when men, or women for that matter, didn't profess
their love in this way. But in the last six months,
my dad sometimes has been saying I love you first,

adds "more" to the end or "I'm glad we had you,"
or on Super Bowl Sunday, when I stop down
for a visit, and after my usual kiss on the cheek,
he says, "I loved you nine months before
you were born."

I couldn't top that one either.

Letting Go

I think back to high school, you taking the train to Manhattan.
After school and on weekends you'd hang out with friends
in Central Park, Union Square, the East Village,
go to concerts in dive bars, ride the subway to Brooklyn
at midnight to take your girlfriend home, then back
to Penn Station to catch the 1:22 a.m. to Hawthorne.
I let go four years ago. I had to,
had to trust, even though I didn't always know
where you were, didn't know what
you were doing. I let go, not little by little,

but all at once, like a balloon leaving my clenched
fingers, swooshing into the sky
within minutes, climbing
higher and higher until it became a bright red dot
in the clouds. I let go, because I made a decision
that your opportunity, your independence,
was so much bigger
than my fears, my desire
to hug you to me.

The Big White House on the Corner

My dad is standing outside his house, the big white house
on the corner of Arlington and McKinley, admiring
his perfectly manicured lawn and his pink azalea, a wild thing
next to the waxy rhododendrons, the ones
with the purple flowers that always remind me
of my mom.

I've lived here for 41 of my 52 years.
I was brought home to this house from St. Joseph's,
played Matchbox Cars with my brother on the cracks
of the sunroom slate, played badminton, Twister and catch
with my dad in the backyard, the backyard
with the wall of red roses and the lilac bushes,
one a deep, deep violet, the other lavender,
so fragrant my mom would cut them off
in bunches, wrap a wet paper towel and tin foil
around the stems, gifts I'd bring to my teachers
at the Catholic school in town.

I played hopscotch and Chinese jump rope
with friends out front on that uneven sidewalk,
played kickball and tag on this street
with my best friend Cheryl, the neighborhood kids
and a bossy girl who sometimes made me cry.

I lived in this big white house on the corner
for three decades, 'til I bought my first place,
a condo in Wanaque. I lived there three years,
spent another seven in Kansas City,
then Chicago because of my husband's job,
before moving back at 42 to take over
the upper floors here, once home to tenants,
when my son was eight,
my daughter almost three.

We didn't intend to stay, but my mom got cancer,
broke her hip and so we turned a one-bedroom apartment
into a three-bedroom. My daughter's room became
what would have been our living room, my son's room,
the renovated attic.

My favorite space became the landing off the back stairs,
with its thin grey utilitarian carpet, its green and white tin roof,
the roof that collapsed this winter in a snowstorm,
the roof that protected us for all those years from rain
and sun during birthday parties and family dinners,
card games and Clue and dancing wild
with the kids and friends on summer evenings,
the roof that protected me while reading or writing
on my favorite loveseat, the one with the blue
and white denim couch cover,
the first piece of furniture
I ever bought.

This big white house on the corner holds
my best memories: getting ready for prom, writing in my diary
flopped on my stomach on my pink-flowered bedspread,
my mom on the sunporch or cooking Christmas Eve
dinners, dinners that seemed to go on forever, those five-course
meals – the antipasto, the salad, manicotti, all that fish, Italian
cookies and pies and cannoli – and my mother's sisters
(Aunt Anna, Aunt Rose and Aunt Helen), all gone now,
and their husbands and their kids, my nieces and nephews,
and how we laughed, back when all of us
and this house were younger.

I came back out of choice,
stayed longer than I'd thought
out of obligation, but mostly,
I stayed out of love,

and even though I've dreamed of living on a horse farm
or in the mountains, at the Jersey shore or in the East Village,
I've stayed here
to be there for my mom, and now
that she is dead, I stay for my dad,
because he always told me, even when I was a young girl,
"You're going to take care of me in my old age."

Now that he is 95 and old age lives here, I stay.

But I don't look forward to the day
when I will once again have to choose
between living
in this big white house on the corner
or leaving it

and how will I ever move away from all
I'd have to leave.

What Is It I Love When I Love You?

What is it I love when I love you? That when
I said I wasn't sure I wanted to move to Kansas City
when we were dating long distance for only three
months, you said, "You don't have to. I'll move
to New Jersey," and you did. You quit your job, a good
job that you loved, but I guess not as much as me,
and you moved all your stuff in a snowstorm and you
got stuck in Pennsylvania and you were up for 36 hours
straight trying to get to me.

What is it I love when I love you? That when I tried
to fight with you early on in our marriage, you said,
"Is that the best you can do?" and I realized
it was no fun to fight with you and so I didn't,
and it's a good thing I didn't marry an Italian.

What is it I love when I love you? That you are
the smartest man I know, though you don't have a Ph.D.,
yet you know something about almost everything
and you can find your way through Newark or Harlem
even though you grew up in small town Iowa.

What is it I love when I love you? That after I introduced
you to my dad on your first trip to Jersey, when we
were all standing on the brick patio outside my house
on that Memorial Day weekend, and I said,
"This is Dan from Kansas City," and you shook his hand
and he said, "I guess, we'll never see you again,"
I did see you again.

What is it I love when I love you? That you are the most
unselfish person I know, you're a good cleaner, love
to cook and take care of the people you love,
and one day when you were talking with my mom
about ironing, something I hate to do, you asked her
about the best brand of irons and she told you
what it was, and told you to go buy it, wrap it,
and give it to yourself from her for Christmas. It was
then that I realized I married my mom
and I was okay with that.

What is it I love when I love you? That when I
became a vegan at the age of 48 and told you
that I loved you too much to ask you to be one, too,
but I wanted you to read at least one book so that we
weren't like ostriches with our heads in the sand,
and if after you read that book you still wanted
to eat beef and chicken and turkey and fish and milk
and eggs that was okay, and even though you grew up
on meat and potatoes and milk straight from the cow
with a layer of thick cream on top, you read that book
and became vegan, too.

What is it I love when I love you? That we went
on a second honeymoon for our 20th wedding
anniversary and watched the sunrise over Haleakalā
and the big sea turtles take an eternity to scoot
on an inky beach made of bits of volcanic rock,
that we drove narrow, isolated mountain
roads on the south side of the Road to Hana,
and even though the scenery was a monotonous
moonscape, I loved being in that car with you,
my hand resting on your thigh,
laughing about the seven pools,
seeing your Midwestern skin that usually turns red,
turn golden in the island sun.

93

ACKNOWLEDGMENTS

W ith gratitude to the editors who have published or will be publishing many of the poems in this collection, sometimes in earlier versions:

PATERSON LITERARY REVIEW

2010: *Imprint*
The Hour
My Father the Limo Driver
2011: *Alone*
Browning Leaves
2012: *Taking the Train to Regis*
2013: *Hot Pink Rubber Gloves*
Love Poem to My Father
2014: *Watching My Parents Dance*
Watching Oprah with My Mom
2015: *The Jeeperettes*
Driving in the Fast Lane
Rain on a Tin Roof

LIPS

2012: *What the Sea Swallows*
Cheap Cologne
2013: *A Midnight Encounter*
2014: *Letting Go*
TBA: *What Is It I Love When I Love You?*

PADDLEFISH, 2012: *Idling*

MEADOWLANDS MUSE, 2013: *The Cardinal*

TIFERET, 2013: *In the Chapel at St. Maguerite's (part 1)*

KOREAN EXPATRIATE LITERATURE, 2014: *The Quiet*

GREAT FALLS: AN ANTHOLOGY OF POEMS ABOUT PATERSON
2014: *Swimming at the Great Falls*

Biography

SUSAN LEMBO BALIK is the Associate Director of Cultural Affairs at Passaic County Community College (PCCC) in Paterson, New Jersey, home to the Poetry Center in the historic Hamilton Club.

Before joining the PCCC staff, she worked as a newspaper feature writer and wrote a parenting column focusing on health, nutrition, environmental and spiritual issues.

She lives on the upper floors of her two-family childhood home in Hawthorne, New Jersey, with her husband, two teenagers and two dogs. Her very independent 95-year-old father lives on the floors below.

She holds an M.A. in journalism from New York University. Her poems have appeared in *The Paterson Literary Review, Lips, Paddlefish* and *Tiferet*.

Sinatra, The Jeeperettes & me is her first book of poetry.